Who's awesome?
You're awesome.

That thing you just wrote—that was awesome.

1-800-You're-Awesome

You're . . .
(wait for it,
wait for it . . .)
You're awesome.

. . . and you're awesome.

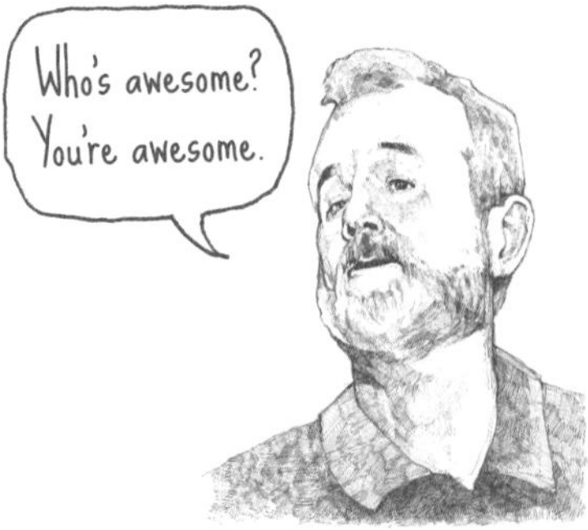
Who's awesome? You're awesome.

#justsayin
You're awesome.

That thing you just wrote—that was awesome.

NO ONE WILL EVER BELIEVE YOU.

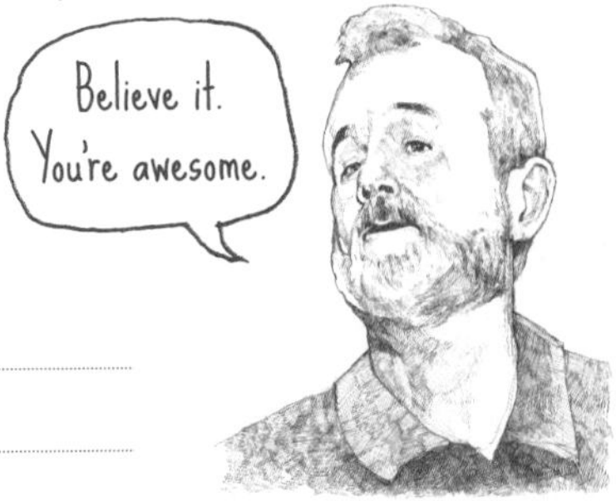

. . . and you're awesome.

Who's awesome?
You're awesome.

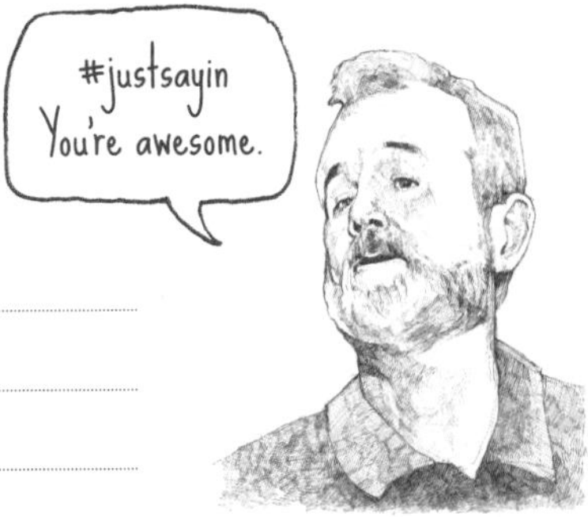
#justsayin
You're awesome.

That thing you
just wrote—
that was
awesome.

1-800-You're-Awesome

You're . . .
(wait for it,
wait for it . . .)
You're awesome.

NO ONE WILL EVER BELIEVE YOU.

Believe it. You're awesome.

. . . and you're awesome.

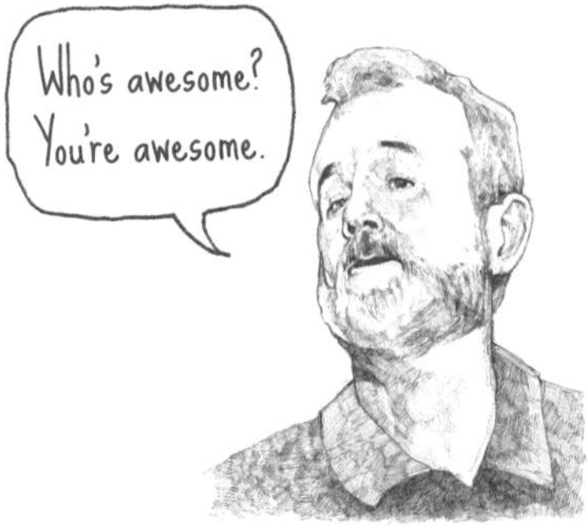
Who's awesome?
You're awesome.

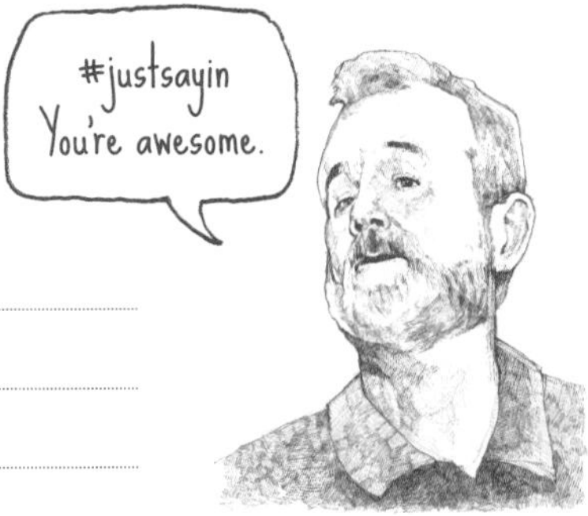
#justsayin
You're awesome.

That thing you just wrote—that was awesome.

1-800-You're-Awesome

You're . . .
(wait for it,
wait for it . . .)
You're awesome.

. . . and you're awesome.

Who's awesome?
You're awesome.

Don't sweat it.
You're awesome.

#justsayin
You're awesome.

That thing you just wrote—that was awesome.

1-800-You're-Awesome

You're...
(wait for it,
wait for it...)
You're awesome.

NO ONE WILL EVER BELIEVE YOU.

Believe it. You're awesome.

...and you're awesome.

Don't sweat it. You're awesome.

#justsayin
You're awesome.

That thing you just wrote—that was awesome.

1-800-You're-Awesome

You're...
(wait for it,
wait for it...)
You're awesome.

NO ONE WILL EVER BELIEVE YOU.

Believe it. You're awesome.

. . . and you're awesome.

That thing you
just wrote—
that was
awesome.

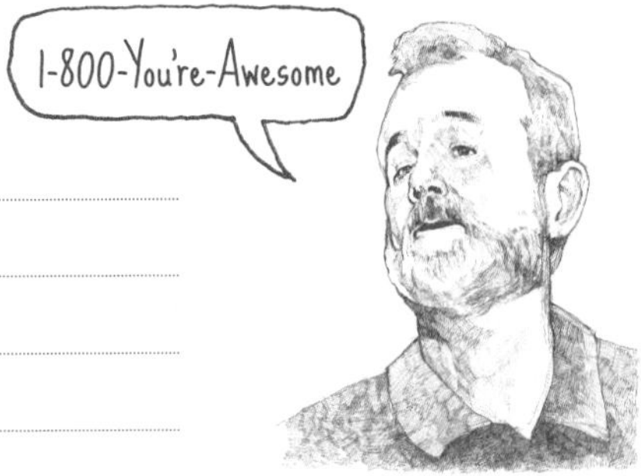
1-800-You're-Awesome

You're . . .
(wait for it,
wait for it . . .)
You're awesome.

. . . and you're awesome.

Who's awesome?
You're awesome.

Don't sweat it. You're awesome.

#justsayin
You're awesome.

That thing you
just wrote—
that was
awesome.

1-800-You're-Awesome

You're . . .
(wait for it,
wait for it . . .)
You're awesome.

NO ONE WILL EVER BELIEVE YOU.

Believe it.
You're awesome.

...and you're awesome.

Who's awesome?
You're awesome.

#justsayin
You're awesome.

That thing you
just wrote—
that was
awesome.

You're . . .
(wait for it,
wait for it . . .)
You're awesome.

NO ONE WILL EVER BELIEVE YOU.

Believe it. You're awesome.

... and you're awesome.

Who's awesome?
You're awesome.

Don't sweat it.
You're awesome.

#justsayin
You're awesome.

That thing you just wrote—that was awesome.

You're . . .
(wait for it,
wait for it . . .)
You're awesome.

. . . and you're awesome.